# The Bridge

by

Alice Barrett

Published by Human Error Publishing
Paul Richmond
www.humanerrorpublishing.com
paul@humanerrorpublishing.com

ISBN: 978-0-9973472-7-2

*Mother Courage: Goshen Barn* was first published in
Compass Roads: A Dispatch from Paradise (Straw Dogs
Writers Guild, Levellers Press.)

Dedicated to Jeannine Haas

My wife, my love, my wise clown.

In memory:

Katie Batters of Emly Parish, Tipperary.

# Table Of Contents

# The Bridge

## Catch the Next Train

If time was a locomotive, I'd catch the next train out of town.
Our town has no train.
If we had a bus station, I'd catch the next bus.
As it is, I'll walk down to the highway and flag a ride.
No, I'm too scared to hitch.
I'll stroll in the woods surrounding the house,
 listen to the leaves chatting.

They ignore me as they chatter away, so I pass by unnoticed,
As I prefer.

My fear is to hear footsteps and a voice hunting for me,
but no one comes.

I hadn't noticed the wind kicking up, swirling up into a
rushing sound.
The leaves panic as the wind like a train rises up and rips the
leaves down.

This, I think, is perfect.

# Listening to O'Carolan

*Turlough O'Carolan, harpist/ composer,*
*born blind 1670, County Mead*

First morning sun pries open the mountain.
Her rays sparkle on the pond and widen
And rush across the field, illuminating sheep
As they pass.

Rays bolt through the open front door and creep
To Baby's bed and rest there for a moment. then
Over to the market, to swirl among the villagers
Already bartering bread.
Light stretches out and out until

Beams waken the hills beyond,
And a swift swallow of lyric sound
Bursts out of all boundaries and swallows
The whole County Roscommon.

What was dark is now covered
With light and cloud shadows racing in circles
Above the meadow.
In evening they lie next to each other
In sweet smelling grass.
They entangle with delight until twilight sends
them slowly back into the ground.

# If I Had a Needle

If I had an needle I'd sing you a song about a dress.
It would be the pretty blue and white one
Mom sent me out to play in.
But, there were benches to climb on
and railings to hang from, so
She gave me bloomers to wear under the dress
    and over my undies.
But I could not hang from railings
because people would think that
    I'd hang from the railings
even if I didn't have bloomers on
        and that would be awful,
        and shame the family.
So I puzzled about why to have bloomers at all.

Or I'd sing you a song about the dress that was blue,
A jumper with a white blouse with a Peter Pan collar.
This all girls wore everyday to school.
Thus began my disinterest in fashion.
And my preference for ease and comfort,
To my mother's dismay.
What beautiful dresses she wore
after a lifetime of hand-me-downs.

How about a song about a wedding dress?
It was white and blue with a beautiful white straw hat.
The maid of honor wore a purple dress and a bridesmaid
wore black.

Dresses I wore are far and few between.

I'm looking for a needle that can slide between events
And clasp them together.
Gather them into a cloth I could cover my present with,
Hold against my cheek and drift off under their weight.

Can I use my grief as a needle and sing a song of loss?
Not about a dress, but about the people who dressed me?

Not about jumpers, but about the friends who touched me?
Not just about dresses,
but all the clothes that embraced their soft bodies?

If only I had a needle,
If only I could sing.

# Dragging My Junk Behind Me

Wherever I go, I'm dragging my junk behind me.
Oh, can't I let it go, let it go.
Oh, can't you see, I'm dragging my junk behind me.

I embarrassed myself loving a girl in eighth grade.
I embarrassed a man in front of a crowd.

I lost my place in an important speech
I forgot my lines in a play, I insulted my father.

I lost a tooth, my own damned fault,
I got hit by a car, it wasn't my fault, but

I'm dragging my junk behind me.
When we go out to dinner
And I stumble to my chair,
Don't mind me,
I'm just dragging my junk behind me.

# Corn

The dark sky churns for hours, refusing
to open.
The sky flashes lightning, igniting a barn, but refusing
to open.
The hard earth shrinks, and like a web across the field,
cracks open.
The dust, the stalks lie open under the clouds, almost as if
straining with hope.
Drops fall, singly, scattered, from clouds
bloated with rain.
Then the dark clouds quiet, pull apart,
dissipate.
And again the sun spreads its heat,
blazing across the cloudless sky.

## I Hate Autumn

The colors, the wind, the chill, the wilted plants.
Autumn is the drama queen of the year,
Always in crisis,
Flinging beauty about recklessly.

Autumn gets under your skin.
Sneakier than winter, more glamorous than spring.
Deceitful, unlike steady, predictable summer.
Your body rebels, gets hungry, dry, tired.
Bones really can get cold.

Hard earth, rotten crab apples, smacked pumpkins,
Cold floor in the morning, hot floor by the fire.
Autumn brings discomfort, irritation, stinky sweaters,
Dark afternoons, garbage tipped over, the cat goes
In and out, in and out, in and out baffled by the cold.

Okay, so the kids scrape through the crunchy leaves.
The dog is friskier, the sky is blindingly clear,
The stars almost touch the garden ground.
The roof stops leaking. No more mowing.

I don't care, I still hate autumn.

# The Bridge in the Woodland

It comes out of nowhere, that bridge,
A rusty, bolted anomaly stretching
Among trees that had devoured the fields plowed before
Metal bridges began.

Along we come,
A brownish Bondo-ed auto that should be a memory, but
Lives beyond its time.

So we arrive at the end of
The unpaved road encapsulated by buckthorn,
Where the bridge begins.

We brake at the edge,
My car and I, who come exploring, nothing more,
As we often do.

Face to face with the bridge,
Flaking bolts, hornet nests in the arch, and foxtail in the girders,
Bridge barely standing, beyond its time,

We sit there,
Engine clanking, spouting exhaust, thinking about options,
Even when there really are none.

I put the auto in reverse,
Three-on-a-tree, forward and up from neutral,
Hook my arm on the seat back.

The road is not as straight as I remember getting here.
Steering reverses in reverse; we swing back and forth,
Skimming the soft gutters.

No springs, no shocks,
The road feels wilder going backwards,
Lunar regolith.

We explore where we've just been, slowly.

Sporadic elms, balding, reach over, hanging
Beyond their expected lifetime.

Jewelweed brushes the car door.
Thick snakes of bittersweet girdle the trees,
And now heat through the metal roof.

Crank down the window.
Black flies and fumes rush in.
Crank up the window.

The clutch slips.
The auto bucks and stalls.
Here. Nowhere.

Start 'er up, first gear,
Gas petal down, spitting dust from behind.
Back forward to the bridge.

Okay, my mother bridge,
Our lives depend on your deck:
Mesh held together by old pitch.

Willing the auto to skim like a skater,
Propelled by speed and second gear,
We let out a scream and go.

# The War to End All Wars

# Here's Looking at You

Sun's out,
hummingbirds are humming.
Then one stops,
hovers.

One eye
stares at me,
staring at him.
He flicks away.

What's his name?

Either
ruby-throated hummingbird,
or the nano Aerolivonment spy drone
which looks and flies
like a hummingbird,
a camera behind its eye.

# What Is New to Me Now

What is new to me now
(don't bother me with cell phones, legalized weed, what the hell?)

What is new to me now is constant war with no intervals of peace.
What is new to me is the eradication of the illusion
That intervals of peace existed between wars.

What is new to me is the eradication of the illusion
That racial justice was within sight.
What is new to me now is the necessity of Black Lives Matter.

What is new is the eradication of night sky and of silence.
New to me is the realization of how much work it takes to make
fleeting gains,
And how fleeting those gains can be.

What is new to me?  the death of unions, global warming,
Fracking, intelligent design (what the hell is that?)

What is not new to me is how little great speeches mean.
What is not new to me is how much poetry means to some of us.
What is not new to me is how much poetry is disparaged.

What is new to me is the sound of my voice reading poetry.

## The War to End All Wars

We never thought we would go to war again.
1914: "The War to End All Wars."
The irony of that title increases over time.
Laughable, if laughable was an appropriate term.

If we fight with computers, is it still war?
Hardly any boots on the ground...
It depends on one's perspective,
Aiming with the toggle or running from the drone.

# Exceptions

I'm a Christian, he wrote,
Except
I'm an eye-for-an-eye kind of guy.

Yeah, I'm Leonardo da Vinci, I said,
Except
I can't draw.

And I'm a pacifist,
Except
When I'm pissed.

I'm a feminist,
Except
Poor women are ugly, right?

I forgive my enemy
Except
Uncle Simon
And what he did to me.

I will give a man my cloak,
Except
Not the nice one from Peru.

We march straight toward freedom, unwavering,
Except...

# How Do You Ask a Soldier to Murder?

Hitler ignored advice and
invaded Russia.
The soldiers who were frightened
were forced to dig their own graves.
Their friends shot them.

"How do you ask a soldier
to murder?" one German soldier asked.

Hitler said,
"For every German soldier killed
one hundred civilians will be shot."

"It was an order to murder.
"There is no other word for it," a German officer said.
"How do you ask a soldier to murder?"

In Vietnam, a lieutenant asked
about the civilians gathered in a hamlet.
The captain ordered,
"Kill anything that moves."

In an ethical war, who can you kill?
Who can you not?
Who are the innocent in a world of enemies?

# Rage

Rage pushes quietly through
the tiger's cage and
strains against the elephant's chain.

Rage seeps up the city street
until the roiling cannot be pressed down any longer,
until the silent pushing and straining
finally breaks away.

Rage, like a torrent in a gorge, has no strategy.
Like a tropical storm, rage is merciless.
And like a storm, it dies.

It leaves behind the city broken.
And leaves behind its ravaged citizens
wandering among flames,

As when a meteor hits ground,
trees for miles around are flattened.
Nothing breathes. Everything is waste.

## When There Was Night

Look up! Endless stars in constant motion, moon shadows,
deep sleep, brilliant dreams, waking dreams, shared dreams,
zodiacal light, blue, white, red starlight, "The Heavenly
Shepard," and see! the footprints of Vishnu!, birds against
the moon, the long, slow spinning of the universe above...

Then, forgive us, we prayed,
"Lead us, Lord, into the light..."
First fire light, then
oil lamps, then
gas lamps, then
electric lamps, and
Night is conquered.

Thank you, God, Tesla, Edison.
Thank you, coal.
Thank you, solar power,
        (we help the sun defeat its enemy night).
Thank you for the ever-present day.

Headlights, neon lights, street lights, reading lights, flash-
lights, florescent lights, desk lamps, spotlights, night-lights...
Half of our life, the beauty of night, crushed beneath light.

# Intolerable

Some mistakes are tolerable,
choosing the wrong job,
going to a lousy school,
spending months writing a bad novel.

Some are not,
not leaving him before he abuses your child,
drinking too much before court appearances,
fighting in jail.

Some mistakes have no safeguard,
not the mistakes themselves,
but where you are at the time,
who is around you,
how desperate you are.

Some mistakes you learn from,
you can turn around,
you can move along.

Some mistakes you cannot learn from,
not in time anyway.

# Catholic High School

They sent us forth under false pretenses.
They sent us forth with the idea that we knew the world,
     knew where we stood,
     knew what needed to be done.

In truth, after graduation, we landed like turnips off a turnip
truck:
     stunned by the world,
     confused by reality.

Some of us stood stock still, rigid in the pretenses.
Others floundered,
Running blindly toward any sacred security.
And what of those trying to collect meaning
As a little boy tries to capture frogs?

And me, dumb as a doorpost,
Hanging onto the strap on a subway car,
Letting the coach sway and shake and screech around me,
     waiting for a stop that looks good,
     getting off for a while to look around.

Each stop has its own smell, its own dirty tiles,
Its own people to walk past as they sleep, in
     Dorchester, Waltham, Roxbury, Manhattan,
     The Bronx, Mexico City, Bangkok, Hanoi....

I settled in a town much like Middlemarch,
     surrounded by flower smells, leaf color, neighbors,
     far from the madding crowd,
     on ground that does not move.

# Death Came Near

# Death Came Near

Death came near.
Death backed away.

She never leaves without a fare-well gift:
Scars, fears, memories,
A limp, a pain, a tremor.

She never leaves entirely,
Like a dimness that never blackens:
Whispers, shadows, shades.

She never leaves forever:
Remember, remember, remember,
She chants in my ear,
softly when the room is quiet.

# The Wound

Rupture breaks through the skin,
Bleeds, leaves a gash, cools.
Comes to rest.

On my back the cooled flow
Creates a ridge, a gap.
I watch the searing glow solidify,
A map of its path across flesh.
I scratch the scab to see inside,
The raw wet pain of my body,

Your body in pain, this thin place,
Where we each live, the wellspring
We share.

## Thin Places*

The scars on my back are my own thin places.
Fragments of ribs float in the empty ocean of my chest.
The plate in my leg bridges yet another thin place

Where eternity entered my body
And nestled beside flesh.
These are the places I carry.

The sacred came and imbedded in this self.
Heaven is resting within my reach,
There to touch when I choose.

Were I not afraid to choose.


*A thin place, from the Celts: where the border between the physical and divine worlds is thinest, where the present moment touches eternity.

## Every Sense

Every sense is losing its grip
Eyes heavy,
Ears ringing,
Rash itching.

When senses finally release,
It's time to sleep, to go
Where all senses are sharp
Alive
And all is bright and singing and clear.

I'm alive in a dream where, if I run fast enough,
I can fly.
If I open my voice loud enough,
I can sing.
Where satin skims across my back unhindered.

# Death House

To this house no trail runs,
No sidewalk riding the earth,
No boardwalk through the cattails.

The windows are not watchful eyes;
They are gaping holes,
Empty darkness with no promise.

The chimney is blocked,
The door is locked, you can be sure
The stairs are unsafe.

What would entice you to enter?
What gain precious enough to brave the door?
For what would you leave safety behind?

A power, a sun, a feather,
A face covered in cloth,
A cage of children?

A dream with no clear meaning,
And no way out?

# Willow Tree

I should've died three times before,
According to how you count, maybe four.
Stand far enough away and it could be six,
(which rhymes with the River Styx).

Now I'm taped together with plates,
screws  and pills, a birdcage
where a ribcage should be,
a peptide hormone injected everyday.

All Zen equanimity dissolved in electrolytes.
Now I am afraid of death.
Not because of what comes after,
An uncomfortable hell or a boring heaven.

No, because now I have plans.
The well-drilling guys tore out my willow tree.
I want to plant a new one and see it mature,
Then sit in its shade.

Now I have plans.
I want to celebrate our twentieth anniversary
And dance there with friends.

I want to travel, though I've never liked traveling,
but this time I'm sure it would be different.

I am afraid of death,
Because now I have plans.

# Architect

To keep a building from swaying
She removed one floor,
The eighty-second I think.

The Chicago blasts can blow right through there,
the building stands firm.
The tenants can walk without wavering.

I could use an eighty-second floor.
Empty, so the winds blow through,
And I can walk without wavering.

# Doorsteps

## That Doorstep

That doorstep trips you up every time.
Look down, the key is under the bucket.
Look up, watch your head.
Watch, don't let the cat out.
Look behind, or the screen door will hit you.

Put your bag down; it tips over.
Look down, the key is not under the bucket.
Look up, bang your head,
Hold the screen with your elbow,
Kick the door with your heel. No one answers.

The cat sits between your legs.

....

## The Stoop

The concrete is hot. It must be summer.
The streetlight sputters on. It must be evening.
The Mallorys slide open their window. There must be a breeze.
Cousin Jimmy has his guitar. There must be no work.
Mom and Mary Ryan sit down to stretch their legs. Dinner must be cooked.
You sit on the bottom step, feet planted on the sidewalk.

A cat sits between your legs.

....

## The Wheelchair Doorstep

Someone must see it is raining.
Someone must be working the door.
It can't be long now, can it?
Surely someone will come soon.

You back up, rev up your arms, and rush the doorstep.
The tiny front wheels catch the lip and tip you forward.
Surely someone will come soon,
See you in the rain outside,

A cat upon your lap.

....

That Last Doorstep

He's lain there unmoving,
Waiting for God knows what.
The nurses lied on his chart -
He has not eaten in days.

His eyes have not opened,
His throat has not moaned.
He's lain there unmoving,
Waiting for ...

He is waiting for the precise moment.
Relax, he's been waiting a lifetime for this moment.
The exact right moment.
Some sound in his silence,
Listening for that precise breath
To choose to be his last,
Before stepping over.

I nestle under his chin,
Feel my purr echo in his chest.

# Saying Goodbye to Eleanor

The hill was quiet except for the wind
The hill was quiet except for our feet, steadily crunching snow

Clouds of visible breath in the frosty air;
No voice, but for a bird we heard calling.

The heavy sled, light with her small body,
Whispered against the trail.

The hill was quiet, just muttered prayers.
It was quiet, silent, even the wind died.

Then a shovel piercing rocky dirt,
Then the loud hollow sound,
The dirt drumming on her coffin,

We watched
As Earth welcomed her home.

We turned back down the hill,
Leaving the silence behind.

# Shattered

for Gregory, 1986

The window glass shattered, and
Fragments spread sun glints over the grass.
Cold breezes drift in.

We can see outside clearly now,
No frosted pane, no steam, no streaks.

You have AIDS now.
We lean over the sill to watch
Glass act like crystal, breaking
The gaseous sun into blinding splints:
      tiny,
      fiery,
      gems.

# What Else He Learned

My restless, fitful cousin
Punched a black patient in the hospital.
At Thanksgiving dinner he offered advice he'd gotten
From a prostitute the week before:
"The best part of sex is right after the orgasm."

One eye had been poked out by a paper clip
when he was in grammar school.
He took a bad trip on spring break in Florida
and angel dust took him to schizophrenia.

His mother woke up one night and saw him
Standing over her holding a knife.
He stands in the living room now, big,
One-eyed, scary. Everyone's left the room
Except my father and me, asking him

what else he had learned.

# The News I Fear

Slugs are not much loved.
Maybe God loves slugs,
But who knows?

One day in the garden, no slugs.
Next day,
slugs.

The invisible destroyer becomes solid,
Well, almost solid;
It's a slug.

Rare is the animal whose name so suits its physicality.

Alzheimer's.
Now there is a name that suits its own ugliness.
Maybe if I was German...

The invisible destroyer becomes solid.
My mother is walking back and forth in her own kitchen
Not knowing where she is.

One day in the kitchen, no Alzheimer's.
Next day...
No, I lie.

Slugs take their time eating away,
Chewing, or whatever they do to petals,
Until one day I notice what is gone.

# When the Snow Dies

When spring comes, the snow dies.
A slow death, gradually buried in mud,
From shining crystal white to muck.
In long shadows, only refugees survive.
For a while.


When spring comes, the wind dies.
Blistering cold overcome by soft, weak streams,
Air that carries the warm smell of earth.
The bracing, awakening clamor of northeast winds,
Gone. For a while.


When spring comes, winter dies.
Again.
The short, brusque days defeated by light.
The stars that break through bare branches,
Smothered now by leaves.

When spring comes, my father dies.
Again.
Bad jokes, the smell of ocean,
A particular conscience, potato chips and beer,
A love he would die for, an IQ too high for his own good;
Too tired to fight, until
Gone. Forever this time.

# Loss

Empty railroad track
Narrows at the horizon's edge —
She died without me


A redhead picks tiny blossoms
From among rocky ruins —
Old monastery far above.


A round daisy chain
Twines the red braids on her head —
It slips as she dances

# Don't Follow Me

Grief is a place that follows.

Turn as many corners as you like,
The same the same the same. Where

The blinding sun never dims,
A dew of ice lies upon everything, and
Light attacks your eyes without blinking.

Doves mourn from wires here,
And gravel cries from underfoot.
Roots and fish-wire snake over the ground.

Only one prayer is left to say,
"Pass me by, just pass me by.
Don't follow me."
Again again again.

## On the Porch

Listen to the quiet between the passing cars.
Listen to the quiet after the neighbors argue.

Feel the rough pod before you break open the milkweed.
Rest before speaking.

Under the blister, soft skin is healing.

Under the noise you will hear
The soft breathing of God waiting
For you to touch Her.

# Home

# A Hundred Ways

*There are a hundred ways to kneel and kiss the ground.*

-Rumi

There are hundreds of ways
to touch a leaf
to hear the sea
Hundreds of ways
to breathe
to sigh
There are hundreds of ways
to touch your skin
to want
to melt.

# When You Said Good Night

It felt like a tug on my skin.
No, my sweet, not like a tug on my arm or leg,
More like a fine layer of skin being pulled off gently,
Or a sheath,
Or a cobweb that had enveloped me.

You will not enjoy being compared to cobwebs
Or to flakes of skin,
With your serious eyes, blue and dark rimmed, worried.
You see, it was not painful,
But was felt
Nonetheless.

Another night I might not have noticed
But again,

Next time, I may touch your arm when you feed me,
Or brush your breast with mine,
Or breathe thank you in your ears
All in the hopes of tempting you to stay.

Know this, my friend,
That whether you stay or go,
As now,
I will sigh with happiness
For you.

# The Taste of the Soul

Morning sunlight melts on the sheets and your legs,
Flows contentedly along your face and into the emptiness of
your mouth.
Like a cat, I smell the heaviness of your breath, lick an eyelid.

My face opens the space between your breasts,
My lips skim through papery skin,
Invisible hair like fur,
My tongue follows the long open bamboo between your
lungs,
Finds ridges and
Space between ridges.

Through your chest my tongue finds
The cave where you beat a slow rhythm.
You wake.
And then...

And then
Brine, salt on smooth cold like
Stones dripping sweat.
Bitter,
Sharp musk like olives,
Salt on lemon, soured bread.
Seaweed, camphor, then
Cedar. The bark catches my teeth.
Then I bite down
Into a rush of wet sweet milk.
What fills my mouth is the taste of your soul.

# More Worms than Dirt

While we were away in the Rockies,
Rains ran down Mount Rood into our garden,
Soaked right in and made the weeds grow high.

We dug our forks in and turned the soil.
Goshen dirt smells good,
Montana has no dirt, just, thin, empty air.

Here each muddy forkful unearths a cluster of worms,
Slimy, lively, fat worms. We carefully pluck them from the clods
And pass them back down to the dirt.

Down inside they burrow around,
Leaving down fertilizer, aerating dirt,
Churning the soil. Like neighbors.

Worms have no eyes, no teeth, but they've got five hearts each,
Plenty to go around. "More worms than dirt," my wife says,
"More worms than dirt."

"I guess they just like it here," I say.
I drop another one under the cabbage,
And breathe in the warm, moist, heavy air.

# Kitchen Counter Love Notes

A-

     At work -
     Sorry didn't do dishes -
     Dog fed
          Cat out -
               Back 6:30
                    Love, J

J -     Went to board meeting -
     Dog is fed -
          Cat out -
   Toby called
          Will do dishes when I get home -
             I love you,  A

A -

     Took dog for walk -
          be back soon -
     Don't know where cat is -
   Sorry about dishes
             Love you, J

J -

     Visiting Mom -
     Took dog -
          Cat outside I think -
     Dishes soaking -
             Watch stupid TV tonight?
             Love you so much, A

J -

     Your sister called yesterday - forgot to tell you
     Dog not fed -
          Dishes not done - sorry -
          Don't wake me up - A

A -

Went to look for cat -
We're out of dog food -
I did dishes except for pots -
Mystery on PBS tonight -
Popcorn?

# Grandma's Friends

Maeve and Hugh came from the Old Country
and didn't smell very good.

My father hid behind a chair
and popped up, "Are they gone?"
while they were still in the doorway.
Mom married him anyway.

With their brogues and silly thoughts,
Maeve and Hugh were like playthings
after they left down the stairs.

Hugh called and asked for Maeve,
"Me?" said Dad. "I'm me, who are you?"
"I'm Hugh."
"No," said Dad. "I'm me, who are you?"
Et cetera, et cetera...

Grandma fed them tea
and listened to their silliness.
They were so far from home and family and good Cashel dirt.

The kitchen floor was covered with newspapers
and at night
she'd roll up the tea crumbs
to keep the floor clean.

# Scotland

I left home with two hats
One blew off
and I came back with five.

One for my ears,
one for my eyes,
one a little too warm,
one a little too small
one, my favorite, ugly as can be.

All well made and useful.
I wish I had five heads.
My wife wishes I had none.

# She Who Is

# Snow

Snow conceals depth and distorts breath.
The landscape of snow is veneer,
      a thin crust pretending to have substance.
I step off the plowed road onto a place with no dimension.
My foot sinks beneath the earth's new surface
      and finds footing on a place I can't see.
The woods across the field are farther away than I had
thought;
With just one step they appear close to me.
.

Sitting in silence like snow,
      depth and breath disappear.
You are farther away than I had thought.
One breath, and You are close upon me.

# Touching the Water

For our ancestors, the wise and unwise

Their blood flows like water through time
And settles for a while in our veins,
Warm and nourishing and
With a long blood memory.

There is no "my blood" to inherit or "my water" to drink,
no "this blood" to shed or "this water" to flow,
Only blood,
Only water.

Only one blood to spill
One water to sail upon

One blood remembering all as it flows through us,
as we struggle to forget.
One water aware of all as it flows around us,
as we flounder in forgetfulness.

The sacred duty for our very brief time here:
Listen.
Remember.
Protect.

# Green Tara

As far as my eye can see —
Green Tara.

Anxious sparrows —
As far as my eye can see —
Green Tara.

Lakes awaiting the storm —
As far as my eye can see —
Green Tara.

Thieves hiding in shadows —
As far as my eye can see —
Green Tara.

Wild moths —
As far as my eye can see —
Green Tara.

Shaking ash —
As far as my eye can see —
Green Tara.

Rapists asleep at home —
As far as my eye can see —
Green Tara.

Restless children —
As far as my eye can see —
Green Tara.

Nightmares and dreams —
As far as my eye can see —
Green Tara
Green Tara
Green Tara

# What It Is

*Beloved, gaze in thine own heart,*
*The holy tree is growing there...*            —*Yeats*

Nothing is just what it is.
Look at that tree.
See centuries of meaning on its bark,
Put there by poets since cave dwellers.

Those meanings stay secret
Without poets. Poets reveal them:
Scribbled on napkins and notebooks,
Composed in showers, in the park,

The poets find longing and history,
Myth and other truths, like yeast in bread.
Look at that tree:
The aching cragginess of its branches,
The leaves shaken off and discarded.

Did you know trees lose their leaves each year
Because one winter, they would not shelter a sparrow?
All except for the pine. Peel that story right off the bark.
Give it to your children to keep. More will grow.

Two monks sat silently
Under a tree, their disciples around them.
Finally, one monk pointed up and said to the other,
"They call that a tree!" And they laughed
And laughed.

# Visions of Jeweled Trees

Visions of jeweled trees are visions.
Visions of dreaming gods are visions.
I have one vision.

With open eyes I see life in quiet stones.
Every pebble sits.
Every green tree sits and breathes.
Everywhere is a great Waiting.
Rage, anger, sadness are everywhere
And everywhere stillness, love and surrender.

# Under the Water's Roof

Under the water's roof the whales sing
Where you cannot hear them.

You can see their backs breaking open
The water and you can remember
The sound.

There's no need to remember Her voice
Singing; it is right there —
The sound of water breaking open.

# Prayer Lesson

Open your mouth to taste Her.
This is prayer.
Open your arms to embrace Her.

This is worship.

Do not shift your eyes from Her eyes.
Do not sound one note in Her silence.

Pray, so that She can taste you.
Worship, so that She can embrace you.

With eyes, arms, and mouth,
Succumb to each other.
This is prayer.

# Black Madonna of Czestochowa

Creation is the fruit of thy womb.
Painful memories and the souls' dark spaces —
The fly in the spider's web —
No suffering is ignored,
No despair unfelt by you,
No grief belittled.

There is no place where Your face does not appear.

# Carve for Me

If I hear Your voice again I shall go mad.
Carve for me a cave in rock.

If I see Your face again I will lose my sight.
Carve for me a cave in rock.

If You should touch me I would burn.
Carve for me a cave in rock.

Carve for me a cave in rock.

# Praise Her

Praise Her who shines forth from each tree.
Praise Her who glimmers on morning grass.
Praise Her who dwells in the breast of the thief and the breast of the
child.
Praise Her who closes Her eyes to no one.
Praise Her who lives as Kali who destroys,
As the Black Madonna who grieves,
As Shakti who dances.
Praise Her.

# Pear Tree

All is grace —
The teardrops of young pears,
The mad wrinkles of tree bark,
The tar on the wound...

The invisible heat,
The blinding glare of the sun,
The damp air...

It is my own frail sight
That cannot look into the sun
Or see into the earth,
And, bound by time, I can only infer
That all is grace,
All is grace...

## I Awoke

I awoke
and found Her arms around me.

My family is Manhattan Irish Catholic. During the U.S. war in Vietnam, I joined up with the Catholic Left and with protest theater, marches, and jailing. Unfortunately, we're still at war. In 1976 Paki Wieland and I went to Ireland to march with the Peace People as they worked to end the violence between Catholics and Protestants. At Thich Nhat Hanh's retreat center in France, I received the Fourteen Mindfulness Trainings (Precepts). I was able to go to Thailand and Vietnam in 2008 when Thich Nhat Hanh returned to his home after exile. During a retreat at Gampo Abbey in Nova Scotia, I emptied to well at the monastery trying to catch up with laundry. I've also gone to meditation retreats at Spenser Abbey and the Siddha Yoga Ashram. Now my home is my retreat; I'm happily ensconced with my wife, my animals, friends, and the forest. The marching hasn't stopped.

I am the House Manager for the wife's theatre production company, Pauline Productions (PaulineLive.com). For years I taught ESL to adults in Holyoke, Massachusetts, and loved it.

My blogs:
poetsindulgence.com
religion-sightunseen.com
dorothytoday.com

16851694R00045